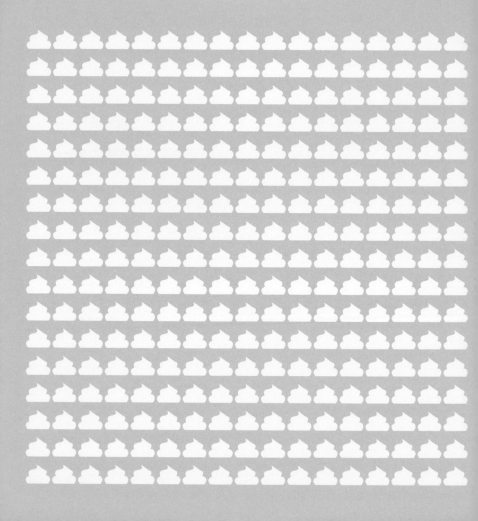

52 THINGS TO LOG ON THE BOG

ALL THAT YOU ARE, LOGGED AND LISTED

HUGH JASSBURN

SUMMERSDALE PUBLISHERS LTD
46 WEST STREET
CHICHESTER
WEST SUSSEX
PO19 1RP
UK

WWW.SUMMERSDALE.COM
PRINTED AND BOUND IN CHINA
ISBN: 978-1-84953-927-2

SUBSTANTIAL DISCOUNTS ON BULK QUANTITIES OF SUMMERSDALE BOOKS ARE AVAILABLE TO CORPORATIONS, PROFESSIONAL ASSOCIATIONS AND OTHER ORGANISATIONS. FOR DETAILS CONTACT NICKY DOUGLAS BY TELEPHONE: +44 (0) 1243 756902, FAX: +44 (0) 1243 786300 OR EMAIL: NICKY@SUMMERSDALE.COM

TO ALL YOU LOGGERS OUT THERE:
KEEP ON LOGGING

TOILET TIME IS REFLECTION TIME. TIME TO LOOK DEEP WITHIN YOUR SOUL AND ASK THOSE PENETRATING QUESTIONS: WHO AM I? WHAT AM I REALLY DOING HERE? AND WHAT ARE MY TOP THREE PIZZA TOPPINGS? WELL NOW YOU HAVE THE CHANCE TO CAPTURE YOUR INNERMOST THOUGHTS IN ONE NEAT BOOK, AND YOU CAN DO IT ALL FROM THE COMFORT OF YOUR OWN BOG. AND THE BONUS? NO ONE WILL DISTURB YOU, UNLESS YOU'RE ONE OF THOSE LEAVE-THE-DOOR-OPEN TYPES.

HOLLYWOOD PRODUCES AROUND FIVE
HUNDRED MOVIES A YEAR. BOLLYWOOD
PRODUCES TWICE THAT NUMBER, AND IS THE
LARGEST MOVIE INDUSTRY IN THE WORLD.

LOG YOUR FIVE FAVOURITE MOVIES →

1 --

2 --

3 --

4 --

5 --

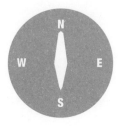

THE NORTHERNMOST CAPITAL CITY
ON EARTH IS REYKJAVIK, ICELAND,
WITH THE SOUTHERNMOST BEING
WELLINGTON, NEW ZEALAND.

LOG THE TOP THREE CITIES
YOU'VE VISITED →

'IT IS A GOOD THING FOR AN UNEDUCATED
MAN TO READ BOOKS OF QUOTATIONS.'
WINSTON CHURCHILL

LOG YOUR FAVOURITE QUOTE →

RIP

ADOLPH BLAINE CHARLES
DAVIDEARL FREDERICK
GERALD HUBERTIRVIN JOHN
KENNETH LLOYDMARTIN
NERO OLIVER PAUL QUINCY
RANDOLPH SHERMAN
THOMAS UNCAS VICTOR
WILLIAM XERXES YANCY ZEUS
WOLFESCHLEGELSTEIN
HAUSENBERGERDORFFWELCHE
ORALTERNWAREENGEWISSEN
AFTSCHAFERSWESSENSCHAF
WARENWOHLGEPFLEGEUNDSOR
FALTIGKEITBESCHUTZENVONA...

UNTIL HIS DEATH IN 1985, HUBERT BLAINE
WOLFESCHLEGELSTEINHAUSENBERGERDORFF
(NOT HIS FULL NAME) HELD THE
RECORD FOR HAVING THE LONGEST
NAME, WITH 746 LETTERS.

LOG THE TOP THREE NAMES YOU WOULD
CHOOSE INSTEAD OF YOUR OWN →

ONE OF THE LARGEST PIZZAS EVER
BAKED WAS 37.4 METRES IN DIAMETER
AND WEIGHED OVER 12 TONNES.

LOG YOUR TOP THREE
PIZZA TOPPINGS →

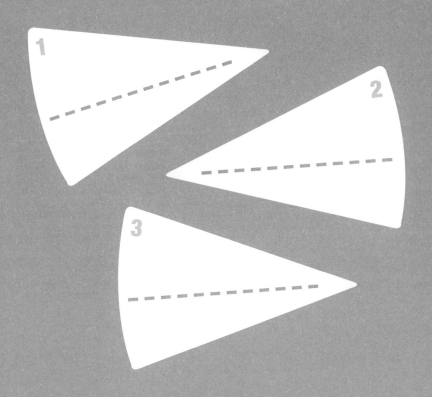

MUSIC AFFECTS DEEP EMOTIONAL
CENTRES IN THE BRAIN, AND CERTAIN
SONGS CAN GENERATE STRONGER
REACTIONS THAN ANY OTHER SOUND.

LOG THE SONG THAT MAKES
YOU WANT TO... →

DANCE

CRY

DO KARAOKE

'ONLY PUT OFF UNTIL TOMORROW WHAT YOU
ARE WILLING TO DIE HAVING LEFT UNDONE.'
PABLO PICASSO

LOG FIVE THINGS YOU'RE GOING TO
ACHIEVE DURING THE COMING YEAR →

A WISE MAN ONCE SAID, 'EXPLAINING A JOKE IS LIKE DISSECTING A FROG – YOU UNDERSTAND IT BETTER BUT THE FROG DIES IN THE PROCESS.'

LOG YOUR FAVOURITE JOKE →

OUR CLOSEST ANIMAL RELATIVES ARE THE
GREAT APES, SHARING 98 PER CENT OF OUR
DNA. WE ALL SHARE A COMMON ANCESTOR,
WHO WAS SWINGING THROUGH THE TREES
AROUND FIVE MILLION YEARS AGO.

LOG THE TOP THREE ANIMALS YOU WOULD BE IN ANOTHER LIFE →

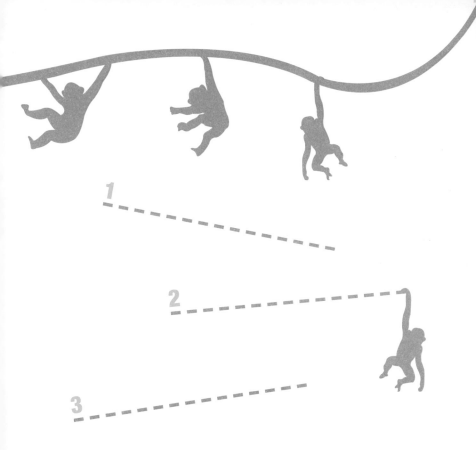

1 _ _ _ _ _ _ _ _ _ _ _ _ _ _ _

2 _ _ _ _ _ _ _ _ _ _ _ _ _ _ _

3 _ _ _ _ _ _ _ _ _ _ _

AS WELL AS RELAXING YOUR MUSCLES AND BOOSTING YOUR IMMUNE SYSTEM, LAUGHING RELEASES ENDORPHINS, THE CHEMICALS KNOWN FOR THEIR FEEL-GOOD EFFECT.

LOG THREE PEOPLE WHO MAKE YOU LAUGH →

FROM A ROMANTIC WEEKEND IN PARIS TO A
ROUND-THE-WORLD TRIP, OVER SIX MILLION
PEOPLE SET OFF ON HOLIDAY EVERY DAY.

LOG YOUR BEST-EVER HOLIDAY →

DATE: _
LOCATION: _ _ _ _ _ _ _ _ _ _ _ _ _ _ _ _ _ _
COMPANIONS: _ _ _ _ _ _ _ _ _ _ _ _ _ _ _

_ _ _ _ _ _ _ _ _ _ _ _ _ _ _ _ _ _ _

ONE OF WALT DISNEY'S HOBBIES WAS
BUILDING MODEL TRAINS. HE HAD A LARGE
MODEL TRAIN SET-UP AT HIS OFFICE AND A
MINIATURE STEAM TRAIN IN HIS BACK GARDEN.

LOG YOUR FAVOURITE HOBBIES →

1 _____

2 _____

3 _____

WHILE CLEARING OUT YOUR GRAN'S
ATTIC YOU FIND AN OLD LAMP.
YOU RUB IT.
YOU KNOW WHAT HAPPENS NEXT.

LOG YOUR THREE WISHES →

1 _ _ _ _ _ _ _ _ _ _ _ _ _ _ _ _ _

_ _ _ _ _ _ _ _ _ _ _ _ _ _ _ _ _

_ _ _ _ _ _ _ _ _ _ _ _ _ _ _ _ _

2 _ _ _ _ _ _ _ _ _ _ _ _ _ _ _

_ _ _ _ _ _ _ _ _ _ _ _ _ _ _ _

_ _ _ _ _ _ _ _ _ _ _ _ _ _ _

3 _ _ _ _ _ _ _ _ _ _ _ _ _ _

_ _ _ _ _ _ _ _ _ _ _ _ _ _

_ _ _ _ _ _ _ _ _ _ _ _ _ _

'I'D RATHER REGRET THE THINGS I HAVE
DONE THAN THE THINGS THAT I HAVEN'T.'
LUCILLE BALL

LOG THREE THINGS YOU'VE DONE
THAT YOU'LL NEVER DO AGAIN →

'HAPPINESS IS NOT SOMETHING READY MADE.
IT COMES FROM YOUR OWN ACTIONS.'
DALAI LAMA

LOG THREE OCCASIONS WHEN YOU
WERE AT YOUR HAPPIEST →

1
--- --- --- --- --- --- --- --- --- --- --- --- ---

--- --- --- --- --- --- --- --- --- --- --- --- ---

2
--- --- --- --- --- --- --- --- --- --- --- --- ---

--- --- --- --- --- --- --- --- --- --- --- --- ---

3
--- --- --- --- --- --- --- --- --- --- --- --- ---

--- --- --- --- --- --- --- --- --- --- --- --- ---

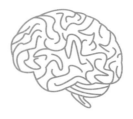

RESEARCH SHOWS THAT OUR FIRST MEMORIES
START FORMING AROUND THE AGE OF THREE,
ALTHOUGH MOST OF THESE FADE BY THE TIME
WE REACH SEVEN OR EIGHT YEARS OLD.

LOG YOUR EARLIEST MEMORY →

'ADVICE IS LIKE SNOW – THE SOFTER IT
FALLS, THE LONGER IT DWELLS UPON, AND
THE DEEPER IT SINKS INTO THE MIND.'
SAMUEL TAYLOR COLERIDGE

LOG THE BEST ADVICE YOU'VE
EVER RECEIVED →

EARLY BOOKS DIDN'T HAVE THE AUTHOR'S
NAME OR THE TITLE ON THE COVERS.
THE COVERS WERE ARTWORKS IN
THEIR OWN RIGHT, DECORATED WITH
DRAWINGS, LEATHER AND EVEN GOLD.

LOG YOUR FAVOURITE BOOKS →

IN OCTOBER 2015, ONE DIRECTION BEAT
THE RECORD, PREVIOUSLY HELD BY THE
BEATLES, OF FOUR SINGLES DEBUTING IN THE
TOP 10 ON THE AMERICAN HOT 100 CHART.
'PERFECT' WAS THEIR FIFTH TOP 10 DEBUT.

LOG YOUR TOP THREE BANDS →

Parkhouse

FROM WORK AND SHOPPING TO GAMBLING
AND CIGARETTES, ACCORDING TO RESEARCH
1 IN 3 OF US ARE ADDICTED TO SOMETHING.

LOG THREE THINGS YOU THINK
YOU SHOULD DO LESS →

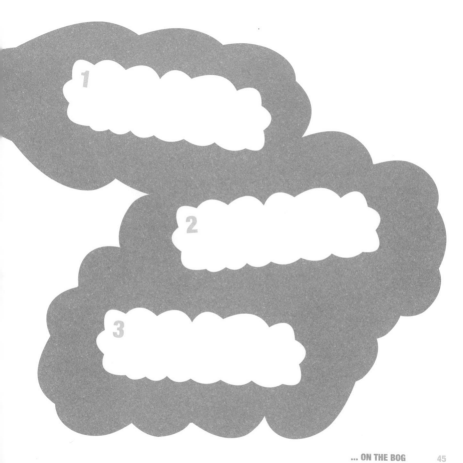

1

2

3

DEAR...

'HINDSIGHT IS ALWAYS TWENTY-TWENTY.'
ANONYMOUS

LOG THE ADVICE YOU'D GIVE TO A
TEN-YEARS-YOUNGER YOU →

DEAR SELF...

_____

_____

_____

_____

_____

_____

_____

_____

_____

THE MODERN PAPER CLIP WAS INVENTED
IN 1899 BY WILLIAM MIDDLEBROOK FROM
CONNECTICUT, USA. TO THIS DAY THERE IS
NO BETTER INVENTION TO FASTEN SHEETS OF
PAPER TOGETHER WITHOUT PIERCING THEM.

LOG YOUR BEST IDEA →

GOOGLE WAS FIRST CONCEIVED DURING A DREAM. LARRY PAGE WOKE UP AND, OVER THE NEXT FEW YEARS, TURNED HIS DREAM INTO THE WORLD'S MOST-USED SEARCH ENGINE.

LOG YOUR DREAMS →

LAST:

_____

_____

_____

BEST:

_____

_____

_____

WORST:

_____

_____

_____

**SELF-AWARENESS IS HAVING A CLEAR
PERCEPTION OF WHO YOU ARE, YOUR
PERSONALITY, YOUR STRENGTHS,
WEAKNESSES, THOUGHTS AND EMOTIONS.**

LOG WHICH THREE WORDS WOULD
BE USED TO DESCRIBE YOU... →

BY YOU:

**BY YOUR
FRIENDS:**

EVEN JUST THINKING ABOUT YOUR FAVOURITE
FOOD RELEASES DOPAMINE, A FEEL-GOOD
HORMONE, INTO YOUR BODY. DOPAMINE IS
ALSO PRODUCED DURING EXERCISE AND SEX.

LOG YOUR FIVE FAVOURITE FOODS →

THE GREEK PERFORMER THESPIS IS
THE FIRST KNOWN PERSON TO SPEAK
WORDS AS A CHARACTER IN A PLAY OR
STORY. IN HIS HONOUR, ACTORS ARE
COMMONLY CALLED THESPIANS.

LOG YOUR TOP FIVE ACTORS →

WHEN THE PHYSICIST AND TEACHER
ALBERT EINSTEIN DIED IN 1955, THE
PATHOLOGIST THOMAS HARVEY REMOVED
HIS BRAIN HOPING THAT FUTURE
NEUROSCIENTISTS COULD DISCOVER
WHAT MADE EINSTEIN SO INTELLIGENT.

LOG YOUR FIVE FAVOURITE
TEACHERS FROM SCHOOL →

1 -

2 -

3 -

4 -

5 -

SIMILAR TO AN ELEPHANT'S TRUNK, YOUR
TONGUE IS A 'MUSCULAR HYDROSTAT':
A GROUP OF MUSCLES THAT WORK
INDEPENDENTLY OF BONES. IF YOUR TONGUE
WAS THE SIZE OF AN ELEPHANT'S TRUNK,
IT WOULD BE ABLE TO UPROOT TREES.

LOG YOUR BODY'S BITS →

BEST: ------------------------------

WORST: -------------------------------

WEIRDEST: ----------------------------

**SPORTS STARS ARE PAID HANDSOMELY,
NOT ONLY FOR THEIR SKILLS BUT ALSO
FOR ENDORSEMENTS. ONE OF THE FIRST
WAS THE CRICKETER W. G. GRACE, WHO
APPEARED ON A COLMAN'S MUSTARD
ADVERT IN 1895 WITH THE TAG LINE
'COLMAN'S MUSTARD HEADS THE FIELD'.**

LOG YOUR TOP THREE SPORTS STARS →

SIR EDMUND HILLARY'S SON, PETER
HILLARY, CLIMBED EVEREST IN 1990,
MAKING THEM THE FIRST FATHER AND
SON TO BOTH SCALE THE PEAK.

LOG YOUR PROUDEST ACHIEVEMENTS →

ACCORDING TO A RECENT SURVEY, SIX IS
THE IDEAL NUMBER FOR A DINNER PARTY.

LOG YOUR TOP FIVE PARTY
GUESTS, ALIVE OR DEAD →

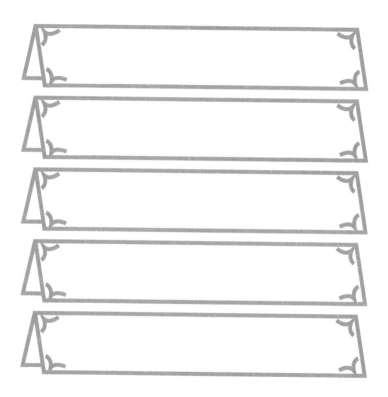

OVER 50 PER CENT OF HOUSE FIRES ARE
CAUSED BY COOKING APPLIANCES. FAULTY
APPLIANCES AND SMOKERS' MATERIALS
ARE THE NEXT MOST COMMON CAUSES.

LOG THE THREE OBJECTS YOU WOULD
SAVE FROM A HOUSE FIRE →

1 _ _ _ _ _ _ _ _ _ _ _ _ _ _ _ _

2 _ _ _ _ _ _ _ _ _ _ _ _ _ _ _ _

3 _ _ _ _ _ _ _ _ _ _ _ _ _ _ _ _

NEARLY FIVE MILLION BRITONS LIVE ABROAD
– AROUND EIGHT PER CENT OF THE UK
POPULATION COMPARED TO ABOUT 0.8 PER
CENT OF AMERICANS, 3 PER CENT OF SPANISH
AND 2.1 PER CENT OF AUSTRALIANS.

LOG THE TOP THREE COUNTRIES
YOU WOULD EMIGRATE TO →

1 _ _ _ _ _ _ _ _ _ _ _ _ _ _

2 _ _ _ _ _ _ _ _ _ _ _ _ _ _

3 _ _ _ _ _ _ _ _ _ _ _ _ _ _

FROM THE TWIRLING SPAGHETTI FORK
TO THE AUTOMATIC WASHING TOILET,
THERE'S A GADGET FOR EVERYTHING.

LOG THE TOP THREE
GADGETS YOU OWN →

MY...

MY...

MY...

'TO SIT IN THE SHADE ON A FINE DAY
AND LOOK UPON VERDURE IS THE
MOST PERFECT REFRESHMENT.'
JANE AUSTEN

LOG YOUR PERFECT DAY →

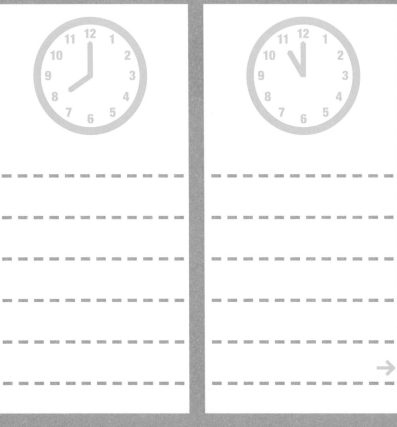

WALT DISNEY INITIALLY NAMED MICKEY
MOUSE 'MORTIMER', BUT HIS WIFE
CONVINCED HIM TO GO WITH 'MICKEY'.
MORTIMER BECAME THE NAME OF A
NEW CHARACTER – MICKEY'S RIVAL.

LOG YOUR FAVOURITE
ANIMATED CHARACTERS →

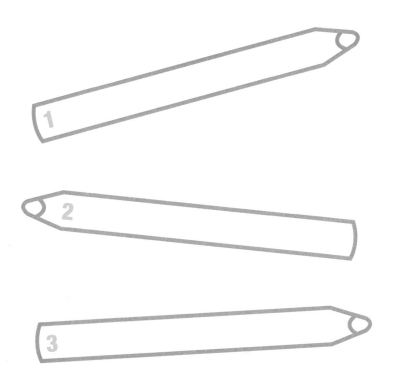

WE ALL KNOW ABOUT SUPERMAN'S
SUPERPOWERS, BUT KRYPTONITE IS NOT HIS
ONLY WEAKNESS. STANDING IN THE LIGHT
OF A RED SUN AND THE CHAOTIC ENERGIES
OF MAGIC ALSO ROB HIM OF HIS POWERS.

LOG WHAT YOUR SUPER POWER WOULD
BE AND WHAT YOU WOULD DO →

POWER:

ACTION:

WITH AROUND THIRTY-SIX MILLION PEOPLE
INHABITING IT, TOKYO IS THE WORLD'S
LARGEST CITY BY POPULATION. LONDON
IS THE MOST VISITED CITY WITH AROUND
SEVENTEEN MILLION TOURISTS EACH YEAR.

LOG THE THREE CITIES YOU
WOULD MOST LIKE TO VISIT →

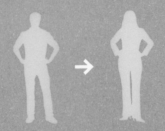

'BE YOURSELF;
EVERYONE ELSE IS TAKEN.'
OSCAR WILDE

YEAH YEAH, WHATEVER...
LOG THREE PEOPLE YOU WOULD
BE IN ANOTHER LIFE →

1

2

3

ALCOHOL IS BANNED FROM THE BRITISH
HOUSE OF COMMONS, EXCEPT DURING
THE BUDGET SPEECH WHEN THE
CHANCELLOR IS ALLOWED A TIPPLE.

**LOG YOUR FAVOURITE DRINKS,
ALCOHOLIC OR OTHERWISE →**

HA!

THE QUEEN HAS RECEIVED ENOUGH ANIMALS
AS GIFTS DURING HER REIGN TO OPEN HER
OWN WILDLIFE PARK. IN 1972 THE CAMEROON
GOVERNMENT GAVE HER AN ELEPHANT CALLED
JUMBO WHO WAS DONATED TO LONDON ZOO.

LOG THE BEST GIFTS YOU'VE RECEIVED →

1 52 Things to
hey on the Bog
book.
10/6/19 - ☺

2

3

A WELL-KNOWN HOTEL CHAIN RECENTLY
EMPLOYED PROFESSIONAL BED WARMERS
TO WEAR HEATED SUITS AND LIE IN
GUESTS' BEDS BEFORE THEY ARRIVED.

LOG WHAT WOULD BE YOUR
DREAM JOB →

£ £ £

ONE OF THE MORE UNUSUAL PURCHASES
BY LOTTERY WINNERS WAS THE HOUSE
NEXT DOOR. THE NEWLY FLEDGED
MILLIONAIRES TURNED IT INTO A PUB.

LOG TWO THINGS YOU WOULD DO AS A MILLIONAIRE →

BETWEEN ON-DEMAND STREAMING SERVICES
AND MONTHLY SUBSCRIPTIONS, THERE
ARE MORE TV SHOWS AVAILABLE AT THE
PUSH OF A BUTTON THAN EVER BEFORE.

LOG YOUR TOP FIVE TV
SERIES OF ALL TIME →

THE SANDWICH WAS NAMED AFTER AN
EIGHTEENTH-CENTURY ENGLISH ARISTOCRAT,
JOHN MONTAGU, THE 4TH EARL OF SANDWICH,
WHO ORDERED HIS VALET TO BRING HIM
MEAT BETWEEN TWO PIECES OF BREAD.
THIS ENABLED HIM TO CONTINUE PLAYING
CARDS WITHOUT GETTING THEM GREASY
FROM EATING MEAT WITH HIS BARE HANDS.

LOG YOUR FAVOURITE
SANDWICH FILLINGS →

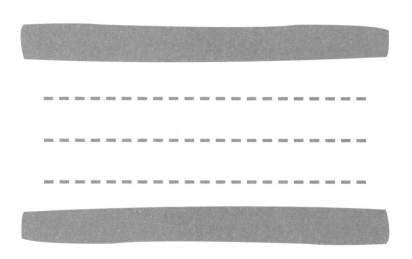

**SOME OF THE SIGNS OF A SECRET CRUSH
ARE A HIGH LEVEL OF EYE CONTACT, POKING
FUN AND MIRRORING BODY LANGUAGE.**

LOG YOUR SECRET CRUSHES →

THE MOST POPULAR FRUIT IN THE
WORLD IS THE TOMATO.

LOG YOUR TOP THREE FRUITS →

1 ------------------------
2 ------------------------
3 ------------------------

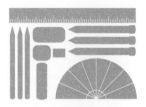

BEFORE THE 1840S, THE ONLY SCHOOLS IN
BRITAIN FOR POOR CHILDREN WERE CHARITY
OR CHURCH RUN. 'RAGGED SCHOOLS' WERE
INTRODUCED IN THE 1840S FOR CHILDREN
WHO, AS CHARLES DICKENS SAID, WERE
'TOO RAGGED, WRETCHED, FILTHY, AND
FORLORN, TO ENTER ANY OTHER PLACE'.

LOG YOUR TOP THREE
SUBJECTS IN SCHOOL →

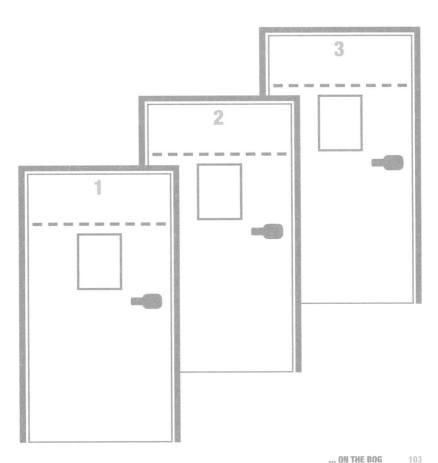

EMBARRASSMENT TRIGGERS THE
RELEASE OF ADRENALINE. THIS CAUSES
THE BLOOD VESSELS IN YOUR FACE TO
DILATE, INCREASING THE BLOOD FLOW
AND MAKING YOUR SKIN REDDER.

LOG YOUR MOST
EMBARRASSING MOMENT →

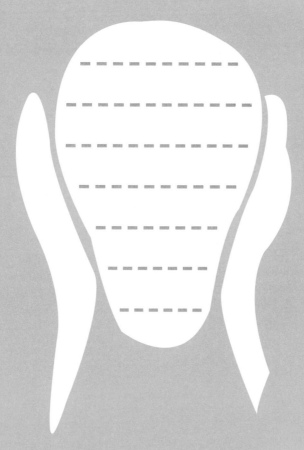

'I AM WHO I AM, I AM WHAT I AM,
I DO WHAT I DO AND I AIN'T NEVER
GONNA DO IT ANY DIFFERENT.'
BUCK OWENS

EVERYONE HAS GOOD AND BAD POINTS.

LOG YOURS →

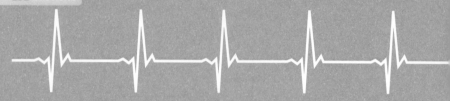

A NORMAL HEART RATE FOR A HUMAN IS
BETWEEN 60 AND 100 BEATS PER MINUTE
BUT CAN MORE THAN DOUBLE WHEN
EXPERIENCING DANGER OR EXCITEMENT.

LOG THE LAST TIME YOU WERE... →

EXCITED:

ANGRY:

SCARED:

YOU HAPPEN TO COME ACROSS A TIME
MACHINE AND PUSH A FEW RANDOM
BUTTONS. YOU END UP 25 YEARS IN THE
FUTURE SITTING OPPOSITE YOURSELF.

LOG THREE QUESTIONS
YOU WOULD ASK →

END OF LOG

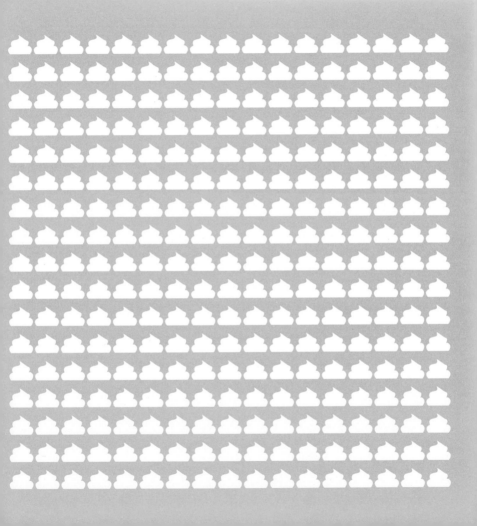

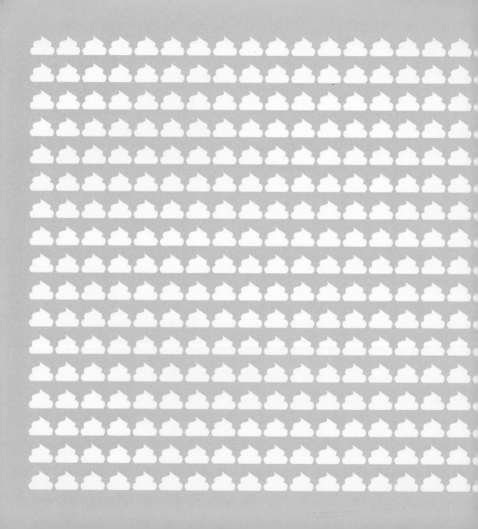